ABBA'S SONG

A Publication of *Tall Pine Books*
119 E Center Street, Suite B4A | Warsaw, Indiana 46580
www.tallpinebooks.com

| 1 23 23 20 16 02 |

Published in the United States of America

ABBA'S SONG

A 49 Day Journey with the Father into Healing, Identity, and Destiny

Sylvia Neusch

The Lord your God is with you, the Mighty Warrior who saves. He will take great delight in you; in his love he will no longer rebuke you, but will rejoice over you with singing.

ZEPHANIAH 3:17

Abba, this book is for You. Thank you for revealing Your Father's heart to me over the years in so many amazing and beautiful ways. Thank you for giving Your only Son, Jesus, that we, Your sons and daughters, can be truly and fully alive with You forever. You are My everything!

Contents

Introduction

THE PAGES OF this book have been forged out of my own journey with Abba. In the Greek language, Abba means *Father* or *Daddy*. I believe each of us has a uniquely personal pilgrimage where we come to know God as our *Father,* our *Daddy God*. Over the years, I have learned to hear His song on the mountaintops and in the valleys. I have heard His song in the barren, dry places as well as the places of refreshing and abundance. Each place where He met me held faceted beauty, revelation, and rivers of healing.

Through it all, the sound of His voice has become the most precious thing to me. Ezekiel describes His voice *"like the sound of many waters..."* (Eze. 43:2b) His voice is assuring, advising, healing, encouraging, and full of His loving heart and nature.

I believe Abba is singing His unique song over

each one of our lives. The prophet, Zephaniah, captures so well the Father's heart for us with these words:

> *The Lord your God is with you, the Mighty Warrior who saves. He will take great delight in you; in his love he will no longer rebuke you, but will rejoice over you with singing. - Zephaniah 3:17*

I trust this book will speak to you as deep calls to deep, but it is not meant to be a substitute for your own journey in hearing Him. Rather, my desire would be that you are inspired to tune your heart to hear His distinctive and personal song to you. The following pages flow in a progression, an awakening journey. However, the writings may be read and meditated upon individually, as well. Each day's writing is accompanied by scriptures, as His revealed word to us through scripture is powerful and essential for our journey with Him.

For those who want to delve a little deeper, you will find something to *ponder* for each day. This may just be the place where the *rubber meets the road,* and you find the needed traction to move forward. The declarations at the end of each day are meant to be spoken out loud, nourishing your own spirit with truth as well as enabling you to sow the words into prayer.

My own heartfelt prayer for you is that Abba's intimate song would reverberate in your own spirit, calling you up higher and deeper into a life-giving relationship with Him. As the Author of your faith, He is orchestrating good things and bringing your life into a powerful crescendo for His glory. Enjoy the discovery and adventure with Him as you listen carefully to His special song to you.

A Seal Over Your Heart

Place me like a seal over your heart, like a seal on your arm; for love is as strong as death, its jealousy unyielding as the grave.

Song of Songs 8:6

I SHARE SECRETS
AND MYSTERIES

MY CHILD, I long to reveal to you the secrets and mysteries of My kingdom. I reveal these things to those who love Me and seek Me just for who I am. You possess a great treasure and inheritance, dear one. It is My joy to journey with you and lavish My goodness on you as your Father.

It is My good pleasure to give to you the Kingdom and I find great delight and fulfillment in watching you discover new realms. The taste is even sweeter when you are thirsty enough to search for a drink. And so it is with My kingdom… as you long for more, the joy of discovery will increase.

I have thrown the door open wide and invited you to step in. Don't be afraid. I will reveal these treasures in time, but you must understand that there is glory in the search and discovery. Don't give up the search! Don't give up seeking Me with your whole heart as there is great joy in the discovery.

I am the *Revealer*, so get ready to be dazzled at what I will reveal. Now, consider how you will cherish the things that I reveal to you. As you choose to steward My gifts to you, they will produce an abundant crop of righteousness in your life and the lives of those around you.

Take a moment to marvel at the wonders I have already shared with you. Savor them as a choice delicacy. Let this *savoring* produce in you a hunger for *more*. There is so much more I want to share with you. Come seek Me, and you will find an unending flow from My throne.

> *The secret things belong to the Lord our God, but the things revealed belong to us and to our children forever, that we may follow all the words of this law. – Deut. 29:29*

> *It is the glory of God to conceal a matter, to search out a matter is the glory of kings. – Prov. 25:2*

Do not be afraid, little flock, for your Father has been pleased to give you the kingdom. —Luke 12:32

PONDER:

Take some time today to meditate on the wonders He has already shared with you. It can be a testimony, a scripture that spoke to you, a healing, or any other encounter you may have experienced with Him. Spend a moment savoring the joy you felt and thank Him that He has more for you to experience.

DECLARATION:

It is my Father's good pleasure to give to me the kingdom.

DAY 2

BE STILL AND KNOW

M Y CHILD, IN My kingdom you are timeless. However, presently you are a *foreigner* living in a world surrounded by time. Remember Paul's words, *"We fix our eyes not on what is seen, but on what is unseen, since what is seen is temporary, but what is unseen is eternal."* (*2 Cor. 4:18*)

When I look at you, I only see beauty. You are Mine—My exquisite creation—My very own. There is no marring that you could experience in this world that could affect how I see you. I see the unseen and find the *temporary* such a hollow picture of the *reality* that I see.

Dear one, comfort yourself in My love, and purpose to explore the depths within Me. I am increasing glory both *in you* and *on you*. My glory brings a beauty that far transcends mere earthly beauty. This is My gift to you.

It is a time to be still and know that I am God. It is important that you align with truth in this new season as everything flows out of that alignment with Me. There is a place of stillness carved out for you as you learn to step in.

You can practice *being still and knowing* when everything around you is moving. This will be your place of peace. This will be your strength.

My winds are blowing. I have heard your cries and the cries of My Spirit within you. Rest in My love, dear one. Speak to your own soul, "*Peace, be still.*"

> *Do not be anxious about anything, but in every situation, by prayer and petition, with thanksgiving, present your requests to God. And the peace of God, which transcends all understanding, will guard your hearts and your minds in Christ Jesus. -Phil. 4:6-7*

> *He got up, rebuked the wind and said to the waves, "Quiet! Be still!" Then the wind died down and it was completely calm. - Mark 4:39*

PONDER:

Today, practice comforting yourself in His love. Allow the cares and worries of your day to roll away, stilling yourself before Him. Remember this mindset, then recall it wherever you are and when you need to experience His peace.

DECLARATION:

Today I will be still and know that He is God.

DAY 3

RECEIVE MY DIVINE EXCHANGE

DEAR CHILD, I am a God of redemption. I have rescued and saved you not because you have earned or deserved it, but because of My great love for you. You are Mine and now part of My family. I want you to receive the Divine exchange that I have orchestrated and planned for you.

Today, I have a crown of beauty for you as you give to Me your ashes. As you release to Me your tears of mourning, I have instead the amazing oil of joy. Where you have known despair, I have provided for you a beautiful garment of praise. Would you hand over to Me your shame, and now receive a double portion? You can now rejoice in your inheritance that is yours through My Son, Jesus Christ. There is no more disgrace for you as He has taken it all away.

I'm asking you to turn over the false identities that you have become so accustomed to wearing, placed on you by the enemy. As you do this, you are not only entering into new freedom for yourself, but you will be a pioneer and forerunner of new freedom for your family. Generations will be impacted because of your "yes" and willingness to trust and receive what I have given for you.

Whatever hand the enemy has dealt you, whether sickness, poverty, betrayal, or any other wicked scheme, I have an "instead of" for you. Lift up your heart to Me and I will transact this Divine exchange with you. You will be established as an oak of righteousness.

Yes, you will be My testimony! You are My planting, and your life will display My splendor. You are My redeemed one and you have a delightful inheritance because of My Son, Jesus Christ.

> *...to bestow on them a crown of beauty instead of ashes, the oil of joy instead of mourning, and a garment of praise instead of a spirit of despair. They will be called oaks of righteousness, a planting of the LORD for the display of his splendor. - Isaiah 61:3*

Instead of bronze I will bring you gold, and silver in place of iron. Instead of wood I will bring you bronze, and iron in place of stones. I will make peace your governor and well-being your ruler. - Isaiah 60:17

PONDER:

Is there an exchange you want to transact with the Father today? Whatever pain, regret, or despair you might have experienced, hand it over to Him. Now receive whatever He has for you instead. (You may want to journal what you experience.)

DECLARATION:

Jesus has taken away all my disgrace and my testimony will affect generations to come.

Day 4

Abiding in the Vine

M Y CHILD, YOU are letting the brokenness and insensitivity of others disrupt your peace. Think of Jesus and how nothing pulled Him off center. You have allowed yourself to be pulled back and forth. I am calling you to learn how to center yourself in Me amid chaos and turbulence.

Learn to recognize quickly when something threatens your place of peace with Me. Peace is My gift to you. It is part of your inheritance and one of the fruits of abiding in Me. Learn to settle into My peace even when you are surrounded by clamoring voices.

Know that you are Mine. Though you encounter a host of relationships in your life, your connection to Me supersedes every other. If you will stay connected to Me, like a grape to the vine, then My life will flow in your relationships just as the nutrients flow through the vine to the grape. It is as simple as turning your heart and affections towards Me over and over throughout your day.

Remember, I have promised through My Spirit to never leave you or forsake you. Apart from Me, you will not experience fruitfulness in any area of your life. You must choose to love and purpose to think the highest and best. If you need to speak a difficult truth, do so in love with the motive of restoration and life for all involved.

Do not let the enemy derail you through offense. Choose the higher road for the sake of the kingdom and My grace and favor will sustain you. If you have experienced hurt and disappointment in your relationships, then release those things to Me and allow My love to sustain you. My love *in you* has the ability to overcome every obstacle.

Now abide in Me. Remain in constant awareness of My Presence within you. I am your safe and steadfast place of sustaining life.

I am the vine; you are the branches If you remain in me and I in you, you will bear much fruit; apart from me you can do nothing. - John 15:5

In your relationships with one another, have the same mindset as Christ Jesus: Who, being in very nature God, did not consider equality with God something to be used to his own advantage; rather, he made himself nothing by taking the very nature of a servant, being made in human likeness, and being found in appearance as a man, he humbled himself by becoming obedient to death—even death on a cross! - Phil. 2:5-8

PONDER:

If you have stumbled in your walk with Him because of offense, receive His cleansing and forgiveness today. Purposefully receive His grace to abide in Him even in the midst of conflict. Receive His perspective for all your relationships and rest in His peace.

DECLARATION:

God desires to bring redemption and life in all my relationships.

DAY 5

EMBRACE MY COAL OF CLEANSING

M Y CHILD, I am restoring My awe to you. I am restoring My awe and the fear of the Lord. I have entrusted you to the Holy Spirit. He is bringing all things into a glorious crescendo and *fullness-of-time season* that will display My glory.

My beautiful one, receive My coal of cleansing as I am perfecting that which I began in you. Arise and shine, for you will be a light to the nations. Your words will flow forth from a sanctified heart and lips that bear the mark of My cleansing coal. In purity and truth you will reveal Me on the earth as the *Desire of the Nations.*

Embrace My coal of cleansing as it is borne out of love and carefully orchestrated for this time and season. My Bridal Army is awakening, but some have not yet sanctified their hearts and lips unto Me. These have not known or been awakened by My love. My love will have its way, as it is a compelling force. Place My love as a seal upon your heart. My jealous love will overcome every obstacle, every hindrance.

I have set doors before you and will open them in My timing. Guard the purity of your heart and the purity of our relationship. What is most precious to you? To what will you give your heart?

All will flow from this place of abandoned intimacy as you give yourself to Me. I am your source. I am your life flow and your place of unending revelation. I am bringing an abundant increase to this place of revelation. I hold the keys and will unlock the doors of destiny for you.

I long to lavish My goodness on you.

"Woe to me!" I cried. "I am ruined! For I am a man of unclean lips, and I live among a people of unclean lips, and my eyes have seen the King, the LORD Almighty." Then one of the seraphim flew to me with a live coal in his hand which he had taken with tongs from the altar. With it he touched my mouth and said, "See this has touched your lips; your guilt is taken away and your sin atoned for." Isaiah 6:5-7

With the tongue we praise our Lord and Father, and with it we curse human beings, who have been made in God's likeness. Out of the same mouth come praise and cursing. My brothers and sisters, this should not be. Can both fresh water and saltwater flow from the same spring? My brothers and sisters, can a fig tree bear olives, or a grapevine bear figs? Neither can a salt spring produce fresh water.
- James 3:9-12

PONDER:

Today is a good day to freshly consecrate to Him your heart and your lips. Ask Holy Spirit to show you how you can guard the purity of your relationship with Him. (You may want to journal what He shows you.)

DECLARATION:

I will guard the purity of my heart and the purity of my relationship with God.

DAY 6

COME ON THE PATH OF PURITY

M Y CHILD, MANY have allowed the pathways of their eyes and ears to be sullied and tainted by that which is impure. This soiling has caused a dulling of sensitivity to My voice. Guard this place of purity with Me.

It is My desire to lavishly pour out My Spirit and bring great healing to you. It is the pure in heart who will see and perceive Me.

Your eyes and ears are gateways. They are the pathways where information, both good and evil, is received. You, along with My Spirit, are the keeper and watcher over your own gateways. Will you consecrate your senses to Me? Will you commit to walk in purity with Me?

My purity preserves, honors, values, protects and cherishes that which is important. My purity increases freedom and allows the unsullied and untarnished life I have to offer you to come freely. My purity is not restrictive, but instead releases the unhindered creative and vast atmosphere of Heaven to you with no hooks or thorns attached.

Understand that it is a day-to-day, moment-by-moment journey and walk with My Spirit. As you walk, in submission and obedience to the voice of My Spirit, purity will be the natural by-product of your relationship with Me.

> *"Keep creating in me a clean heart. Fill me with pure thoughts and holy desires, ready to please you. May you never reject me! May you never take from me your sacred Spirit! Let my passion for life be restored, tasting joy in every breakthrough you bring to me. Hold me close to you with a willing spirit that obeys whatever you say. Then I can show other guilty ones how loving and merciful you are. They will find their way back home to you, knowing that you will forgive them. Psalm 51:10-13, TPT*

> *Blessed are the pure in heart, for they will see God. - Matthew 5:8*

Since, then, you have been raised with Christ, set your hearts on things above, where Christ is seated at the right hand of God. Set your minds on things above, not on earthly things. For you died, and your life is now hidden with Christ in God. - Colossians 3:1-3

PONDER:

Have you ever experienced an increase of freedom from walking in purity? Thank Him today for the grace to walk in purity and the life of freedom without "hooks or thorns" attached, that only He can offer.

DECLARATION:

I gladly receive the freedom, life, and joy that comes from walking in purity with the Spirit of God.

DAY 7

MY CALL TO DEVOTION

M Y CHILD, I am looking for those who will
give themselves fully to Me, those who feel
and hear My call burning within, and those who
surrender the right to their life to Me. My servant
Samuel was such a man. Samuel lived among evil,
yet He remained devoted to Me in the midst of it.
Samuel represented My goodness, holiness, and
purity as he lived among a people who had no
heart for Me or My ways.

Would you be willing to be a *Samuel* in this
generation? This is not a difficult burden, but a
glorious privilege. It is a joyful place of discovery
and intimacy.

When Samuel first heard My voice, he was
lying down in the temple where the ark of God

remained. My very presence dwelled within the ark, and this was Samuel's first encounter. It is also from this place of rest near My presence that *you* are learning to dwell. And, just as I taught Samuel how to recognize and steward My voice, I am teaching you as well.

Would you set yourself apart for Me and surrender to Me your senses? Give to Me your ears, your eyes, your nose, mouth and hands. I have upgrades for you in the prophetic realm as you give your senses over to Me.

When you choose to walk in humility and purity before Me, I am able to expand your influence as I did with Samuel. As you consecrate yourself to Me, I will teach you how to use your gifts to bless a generation for My glory.

Come, rest in My presence.

A third time the LORD called, "Samuel!" And Samuel got up and went to Eli and said, "Here I am; you called me." Then Eli realized that the LORD was calling the boy. So Eli told Samuel, "Go and lie down, and if he calls you, say, "Speak, LORD, for your servant is listening." So Samuel went and lay down in his place. The LORD came and stood there, calling as at the other times, "Samuel! Samuel!" Then Samuel said, "Speak, for your servant is listening." - I Samuel 3:8-10

The LORD was with Samuel as he grew up, and he let none of Samuel's words fall to the ground. - I Samuel 3:19

PONDER:

Consecrate your senses to Him today giving Him your eyes, ears, nose, mouth, and hands as instruments for Him to use. Thank Him for the upgrades in the prophetic realm that He has for you.

DECLARATION:

God is teaching me to recognize His voice and steward His Presence.

LEANING ON MY BELOVED

Who is this coming up from the wilderness leaning on her beloved?

SONG OF SONGS 8:5

DAY 8

WELCOME MY HEALING OIL

MY CHILD, I am healing your scars and re-moving the sting of your past trauma. The enemy has sought to discourage you with his continual taunts and lies. But be of good cheer! I will pour my soothing healing oil into the deepest, darkest crevices of your heart—the places where you have hidden your pain.

There is no need to hide, for My love sees and overcomes all. Come and bring your pain to Me, dear one. I will suture your wounds so that healing will come.

I will seal your wounds with My healing oil. There is healing in My sealing. As I seal your wounds, I will heal the memory of the pain. I am erasing the enemy's recordings and replacing them with intimate encounters with My truth. My truth will set you free to live again.

I am healing first and then revealing. In time, I will reveal the things I have positioned for you. But, healing first, then revealing.

Come and experience My embrace where heart flows into heart. My life flowing into you will realign everything. That which the enemy has meant for evil I am now shifting for good.

This is My promise to you as you bring to Me your "all things." I will work your "all things" together for good because you are My child, My *called one* according to My purposes.

Your heart must no longer be burdened down with unnecessary weights. I'm giving you a heart that soars; a whole heart, a healed heart.

> *He gives strength to the weary and increases the power of the weak. Even youths grow tired and weary, and young men stumble and fall; but those who hope in the LORD will renew their strength. They will soar on wings like eagles; they will run and not grow weary; they will walk and not be faint. - Isaiah 40:29-31*

> *He has sent me to bind up the brokenhearted, to proclaim freedom for the captives and release*

from darkness for the prisoners, to proclaim the year of the LORD's favor and the day of vengeance of our God, to comfort all who mourn and provide for those who grieve in Zion--...- Isaiah 61:1b-3a

PONDER:

Are you experiencing a healing process with Him right now? It's a good day to realize that He is the Healer and His intentions towards you are redemptive and restorative. Spend some time just enjoying His presence today as your Healer.

DECLARATION:

God will heal my wounds and restore me to wholeness.

DAY 9

NEW LIFE IN THE BROKEN PLACES

MY CHILD, WATCH as the fog lifts from your battlefield, giving you a clearer view of the enemy you have faced. The darkness and haze have served as a cover for the evil schemes against you, but My light is burning off the clouds and you will once again see with accurate perception.

He who masquerades as an angel of light will now be exposed for the true darkness he is. Come and bring Me your wounded heart. I will breathe new life into the broken places. Your heart is to be wholly Mine, *holy*, not *holey*.

As you come to Me, I will fill the *holey* places with My compassionate love. I will restore innocence and childlikeness as you taste and see that

I am good. Encounters with My love will erase the painful wounds that have afflicted and hardened your heart and soul. Come now and rest in My perfect intent towards you.

Allow My cleansing breakers to wash over you as you immerse in My goodness, faithfulness, mercy and peace. Now release all bitterness, anger, fear, and regret as they roll farther and farther away in the tides of my great grace.

I am restoring trust where you have experienced confusion and bewilderment. Be assured of this, I am your Defender, your Anchor, fixed and immovable. My hope inside of you will rise, higher and higher, displacing every foreign thought that stands against My Kingdom of Light.

Come away dear one, and rest in the grassy fields of My grace. Be strengthened in My unending, unconditional and unfathomable love for you.

But everything exposed by the light becomes visible—and everything that is illuminated becomes a light. This is why it is said: "Wake up, sleeper, rise from the dead, and Christ will shine on you." - Ephesians 5:13-14

For he has rescued us from the dominion of darkness and brought us into the kingdom of the Son he loves, in whom we have redemption, the forgiveness of sins. - Colossians 1:13-14

PONDER:

Find a quiet place today and lie down in His presence. Allow His cleansing breakers to wash over you, rolling away bitterness, anger, doubt, fear, and regret. Then allow the tides of His goodness and grace to release to you His goodness, mercy, and grace.

DECLARATION:

My hope will rise higher and higher because I am a child of the King of Light.

Day 10

New Vision for a New Season

M Y CHILD, I have seen your hunger and heard your cries for more. This is the time of your visitation. This is the time of your increase. I am equipping you with a new vision, for a new season.

Discard the lenses of your past season for they are no longer adequate. Fresh vision is upon you! This is a time of great transition. This is a time of adjustment. For you will see with *new* eyes and perceive with *new* lenses. I have upgrades for your discernment, and I am lifting you to a higher perspective.

We are going up to a new level, a higher level. Here, you will have an advantage over your enemies. I will give you a *bird's eye view*, a view from above. My grace will come with this shift in perspective.

I am installing a new operating system for a new season. Listen for My direction and set aside past methods and past viewpoints to prepare for the new. Make way for Me as I unveil the new.

You who have grown weary and dull in the waiting, awaken to the stirring of My winds of change. I am blowing even now, removing scales from your eyes and calluses from your heart.

That which you have longed for is upon you. Trust Me as we move to a higher level. Let go of the old ways, the familiar ways and step with Me into the new. Receive your new eyes for the new season.

> *This is why I speak to them in parables: "Though seeing, they do not see; though hearing, they do not hear or understand."- Matt. 13:13*

> *But blessed are your eyes because they see, and your ears because they hear. For truly I tell you; many prophets and righteous people longed to see what you see but did not see it, and to hear what you hear but did not hear it.*
> *- Matt. 13:16-17*

Forget the former things; do not dwell on the past. See, I am doing a new thing! Now it springs up; do you not perceive it? I am making a way in the wilderness and streams in the wasteland. - Isaiah 43:18-19

PONDER:

Receive today the new lenses He has for your new season. Receive the grace and empowerment He has for you in this shift.

DECLARATION:

God is equipping me with new vision for the new season.

Day 11

Lift Up Your Eyes

M Y CHILD, FEAR is not your portion. I have called you to operate according to a different perspective. You are not of this world as your Spirit has been made alive in Me. I'm calling you to come up higher and lay hold of a new way of seeing and being. This is your inheritance in Me. Your worldly, natural view cannot see or grasp what is possible in Me, but as you operate in the power and fullness of My Spirit you will see and know in a new way.

You must *choose* to see with new eyes.

Fear wants to pull you in, to cut off your lifeline of grace in Me and replace it with emptiness, lack, and utter darkness. Lift up your eyes, dear one! I have new horizons and vistas in the Spirit realm for you to see and explore. There is a place for you to dwell above the clamor and pressing evil all around you.

You must focus to find Me when there are so many things vying for your attention. Seek Me and I will be found. I long to meet you in the quiet moments of solitude, but seek Me in the noisy bustle of your day as well. Over and over, direct your attention to the oneness we share.

My glory dwells in you and flows as a refreshing river when you take the time to drink. Purpose to uncap the wells of My Spirit within you. Remove every hindrance, every barrier that would hinder the flow of My river within you. As you rest and flow with My river you will experience renewed vision and hope for the days ahead. Today, see with new eyes.

> *Lord, you alone are my portion and my cup; you make my lot secure. The boundary lines have fallen for me in pleasant places; surely I have a delightful inheritance. - Psalm 16:5-6*

> *I lift up my eyes to the mountains—where does my help come from? My help comes from the LORD, the Maker of heaven and earth. - Psalm 121:1-2*

On the last and greatest day of the festival, Jesus stood and said in a loud voice, "Let anyone who is thirsty come to me and drink. Whoever believes in me, as Scripture has said, rivers of living water will flow from within them."- John 7:37-38

PONDER:

Practice acknowledging His constant presence with you as you go about your day. Thank Him that your spirit has been made alive in Him and given you a higher perspective.

DECLARATION:

God is giving me renewed hope and vision as I drink from His refreshing river.

DEEP CALLS TO DEEP

M Y CHILD, I have walked with you through this season of pressure and fervent yearning. I have planted My seeds of *more* deep within you. You have felt the pull of Heaven's realms in your spirit, calling, urging, and declaring the greater things. Yes, My deep calls to deep within you.

You have felt a holy dissatisfaction with the status quo. You have come this far, and now you know you cannot go back. You have been made for more and the *revealing* is upon you. There has been much preparation to bring you to this moment in time.

You have felt the sting of circumstances and the vice of squeezing that has pushed you through, preparing you for the new. Nothing has been wasted. Every evil assignment of your adversary I am turning. I am turning them for your good and for your favor. They will now serve as stepping stools to propel you higher into your destiny.

I am bringing healing to you now. In this next season, healing will come to your heart as joy and fulfillment erase the pain of your past season. I am shining truth into every dark corner of your heart and mind where lies have hidden until now.

Do not give up hope or abandon ship now, as you are approaching the shores of the new things I have prepared for you. You, along with My Spirit, have navigated well through the tumultuous waters of uncertainty and obstacles. Rejoice, now, as you anticipate and approach your promised lands of inheritance.

> *We are hard pressed on every side, but not crushed; perplexed, but not in despair; persecuted, but not abandoned; struck down, but not destroyed. - 2 Cor. 4:8-9*

> *Deep calls to deep in the roar of your waterfalls; all your waves and breakers have swept over me. - Psalm 42:7*

PONDER:

Have you felt a holy dissatisfaction with things as is? Thank the Holy Spirit for His work in your life to prepare you for what is yet to come. Thank Him that He can use what the enemy meant for evil and turn it for good.

DECLARATION:

The truth of God is transforming my mind and heart.

.

HEALING, THEN THE REVEALING

MY CHILD, DO not hurry through the healing hallways, as the depth of your healing will determine the height of your flight. You will emerge with wings that soar. I am giving you a steadfast heart and I am causing you to rise above those things that have sought to hold you back.

Revelation will come to the *orphan places* still in your heart, revealing true adoption as my beloved child. That which has been masked, covered, and just beyond grasp will all become increasingly clear in glorious encounters with My love.

My child, I am excited that the time of your unveiling is nearing! You are My *workmanship* that I have lovingly labored to create, and I am pulling back the veil that has covered you.

I have painted every season of your life with the utmost love and creativity. The time of unveiling is near, and you will witness firsthand My delight in revealing My masterpiece. Like a well-worded poem, you will emerge, born of My mind and heart, fashioned to impact the world that I love.

The birthing time of My promises is almost upon you. All that I have planned and prepared will be unveiled.

It is almost time for your reveal party, My beautiful one!

We have become his poetry, a re-created people that will fulfill the destiny he has given each of us, for we are joined to Jesus, the Anointed One. Even before we were born, God planned in advance our destiny and the good works we would do to fulfill it! - Ephesians 2:10 TPT

No longer will they call you Deserted, or name your land Desolate. But you will be called Hephzibah, and your land Beulah; for the LORD will take delight in you, and your land will be married. - Isaiah 62:4

PONDER:

What things in your life or experience have sought to hold you back from advancing in who you are called to be? Receive your wings to rise above those things today and review your promises He has given to you.

DECLARATION:

I am God's workmanship, and He delights in me.

DAY 14

I AM THE SKILLFUL VINEDRESSER

MY CHILD, YOU are experiencing a time of preparation, purifying, and crushing. I am preparing my new wine in you. I am awakening love, passion, and purpose deposited directly in you from heaven. As you yield and fully abandon your heart to Me, I will shape and mold you to be a new wineskin ready to house the free-flowing fountain of the new wine of My Spirit.

I am the skillful Vinedresser. I know what it will take in you to create the finest and sweetest wine. I know exactly when it is time to prune your branches to cause increase, expansion, and greater fruitfulness.

You may have felt the pain of the process, and

sometimes felt confused at the cutting away of things that seemed good. Know this My child, My love for you is behind all of it.

Will you trust Me? Will you allow Me to have My full way with you? You have longed and cried out for significance and effectiveness. My beloved, your outward effect will only be in proportion to the inward effect you have allowed and welcomed in your life.

You are in a time of great change and transition. I am creating a new wineskin that will readily contain the new wine of My Spirit. Keep your eyes on Me and trust My hand on your life.

I am the skillful Vinedresser, and you will be amazed at what I will do in you.

No one sews a patch of unshrunk cloth on an old garment. Otherwise, the new piece will pull away from the old, making the tear worse. And no one pours new wine into old wineskins. Otherwise, the wine will burst the skins, and both the wine and the wineskins will be ruined. No, they pour new wine into new wineskins
Mark 2:21-22

Let him smother me with kisses—his Spirit-kiss divine. So kind are your caresses, I drink them in like the sweetest wine! Your presence releases a fragrance so pleasing—over and over poured out. For your love-

ly name is "Flowing Oil." No wonder the brides-to-be adore you. Draw me into your heart. We will run away together into the king's cloud-filled chamber. - *Song of Songs 1:2-4 TPT*

PONDER:

Do you trust Him as your vinedresser? Talk to Him honestly today about where you are in the process of being pruned for greater fruitfulness.

DECLARATION:

I gladly yield to the skill and heart of my Father, the Vinedresser.

CONSIDER HIM FAITHFUL

And by faith even Sarah, who was past childbearing age, was enabled to bear children because she considered him faithful who had made the promise.

HEBREWS 11:11

DAY 15

O MAGNIFY ME

M Y CHILD, THERE is power in what you magnify. That is why speculation is so detrimental for you. When you speculate, you magnify the enemy's plans for you and empower him to access and attack you.

When you choose to magnify Me, everything shifts, though you may not always realize or see it immediately. When you magnify Me, your faith is released, and Heaven is moved by faith. When you choose to magnify Me, your problem grows smaller, and I grow larger.

I am not asking that you deny the reality that you have a problem, rather simply that you magnify Me in the midst of it so that your view of Me is always greater than the problem.

I long to impart to you My perspective. I am always ready to reveal, but you do not always see. Your experience has sometimes taught you things about Me that are untrue. My truth will come by revelation. Open yourself today to receive a new perspective.

You can put the things you receive from Me to the test. Does it look like love? Does it bring peace? Does it increase joy? You must understand, My kingdom is so very different from your present world.

Do not condemn yourself because I do not. When I come, I bring courage, hope, love, peace, and joy. I don't come to punish or condemn. See, My hand is extended to you even now to lift you up to a new place. Will you let me?

Oh, magnify the Lord with me, and let us exalt His name together. I sought the LORD, and He heard me, and delivered me from all my fears. They looked to Him and were radiant, and their faces were not ashamed. - Psalm 34:3-5 NKJV

Finally, brothers and sisters, whatever is true, whatever is noble, whatever is right, whatever is pure, whatever is lovely, whatever is admirable—if anything is excellent or praiseworthy—think about such things.

Whatever you have learned or received or heard from me, or see in me—put it into practice. And the God of peace will be with you. - Philippians 4:8-9

PONDER:

As you spend time with God today, bring before Him any concerns or things that are troubling you. Begin to magnify Him and then ask that He reveal His perspective. Did you see or experience something you have not seen or understood before? Could you make this practice a lifestyle?

DECLARATION:

God is able to reveal to me His perspective as I choose to magnify Him.

DAY 16

MY CHERISHED ONE

M Y CHILD, YOU have forgotten that you are cherished. I do not have it in my heart to abandon My children. I watch over your days, past, present, and future. Imagining the future without Me will always produce a dismal picture. I have you hemmed in, surrounded by My goodness.

Do not question or ponder your inadequacies. My anointing for you will cover you. Where breakthrough is needed—it will come. The Dove of God has come and will rest on you. I will see My plans and purposes fulfilled in you as He works in and through you.

Remember, in My Spirit you go from glory to glory in an ever-increasing likeness to My Son. Lift up your eyes. Your help comes from Me. Your outlook is bright.

If you are struggling in your faith, and faith works through love, then you need a greater encounter with My love. You sometimes feel detached and alone in your fight when all along I have so much more for you. I am here with arms open wide to hold you during your storms. I am your refuge and I have not forgotten you. Today, lean into My strength, and drink deeply of the life I freely offer. Though you may not always see, I am fighting for you. My love for you is fierce and I will contend with those who contend with you.

Let your heart find its true home in Me, then, all the chaos around you will not affect your peace. Know that you are deeply loved and cherished by Me. If that thought is hard to imagine, then you are living short of the love and favor that is yours as My beloved child. Come, snuggle in close. I am your Abba, and you are the apple of My eye.

There are days to pick up your sword and fight, and there are days to run into My arms as I fight for you. Find your place in My arms today. It is a day to trust and come as a child.

The LORD your God in your midst, The Mighty One, will save; He will rejoice over you with gladness, He will quiet you with His love, He will rejoice over you with singing. - Zephaniah 3:17 NKJV

...I have loved you with an everlasting love; I have drawn you with unfailing kindness. - Jeremiah 31:3b

But this is what the LORD says: "Yes, captives will be taken from warriors, and plunder retrieved from the fierce; I will contend with those who contend with you, and your children I will save."- Isaiah 49:25

PONDER:

Today, spend some time just thinking about the reality that you are cherished. Ask the Father to show you what that means. Come as a child and just enjoy His presence and delight in you.

DECLARATION:

My Abba Father deeply loves and cherishes me.

Day 17

Trust Me in the Process

M Y CHILD, IF you find doors closed in front of you it is because I have not opened them yet. I am calling you to a journey of faith. Don't despair over closed doors because there is preparation happening behind the closed doors that will cause the opening to seem even more significant when it occurs.

If it seems that I am quiet, it may be because I have already spoken or because I am inviting you to come in closer. Your fear of disappointment is causing you to miss the joy of abandoned faith in this moment.

If I want something to be revealed, it will be revealed. Trust Me in the process, child, and be faithful with the small beginnings. Watch patiently for the open doors and then walk through them when I open them.

It is not too early to celebrate this victory that I have promised you. Celebrating after the victory requires no faith though a celebration can still take place. This place of *uncertainty* is the perfect altar for a sacrifice of praise. Your lavish praise will open gates and break down barriers. It is the seed of the breaker anointing and the very substance of things not yet seen.

Miriam danced after she saw the parting of the Red Sea and Israel's deliverance. I am calling you to dance *before* you see the victory. This faith-filled dance will break open something new in you and for those around you.

Trust Me in the process. I am creating fruit that will last.

Then Miriam the prophet, Aaron's sister, took a timbrel in her hand, and all the women followed her with timbrels and dancing. Miriam sang to them: "Sing to the LORD, for he is highly exalted. Both horse and driver he has hurled into the sea." - Exodus 15:20-21

The One who breaks open the way will go up before them; they will break through the gate

and go out. Their King will pass through before
them, the LORD at their head. - *Micah 2:13*

PONDER:

Are you experiencing any "closed doors" in your life? What preparation process could you partner with Holy Spirit in as you wait?

DECLARATION:

My God will open doors for me when the time
is right.

Day 18

Keep Your Eyes on Me

M Y CHILD, YOUR hesitation has revealed your unbelief. Did you not know that My strength would be made perfect in your weakness? You have reasoned with your natural mind in an area that can only be navigated by the Spirit.

You are launching out into unknown waters. Though you cannot see what lies ahead or predict the wind and the waves, you can keep your eyes on Me.

You cannot *white-knuckle* your way into the kind of faith that you need. Instead, there must be a childlike letting go and a total trust in My goodness and heart for you as your Father.

Let go of the things that you hold onto, for they are a false security. I am pleased that you are not letting fear dictate your choice to step out. Now watch the words of your mouth and your agreements. Guard this pathway of transaction. Don't give the enemy the benefit of this toehold of access in your life.

I will be blessed with your choice to trust. Make sure you trust big! You will know you are trusting big when the size of the assignment seems too large for you. It will not be something you can accomplish in your own strength. Lean into Me and receive the grace I am releasing today. My angels will assist you and My kingdom plans through you. Dream big! Trust big!

I am pleased with your growth and development. Now throw your caution to the wind and My Spirit will blow it away even further. Remember, I am with you always and I have overcome the world. Come and take your seat with Me. It is your rightful place of intimacy and authority.

Shortly before dawn Jesus went out to them, walking on the lake. When the disciples saw him walking on the lake, they were terrified. "It's a ghost," they said, and cried out in fear. But Jesus immediately said to them: "Take courage! It is I. Don't be afraid." "Lord, if it's you," Peter replied, "tell me to come to you on the water." "Come," he said. Then Peter got down out of the boat, walked on the water and came toward Jesus. But when he saw the wind, he was afraid and, beginning to sink, cried out, "Lord, save me!" Immediately Jesus reached out his hand and caught him. "You of little faith, he said, "why did you doubt?" Matthew 14:25-31

But he said to me, "My grace is sufficient for you, for my power is made perfect in weakness." Therefore I will boast all the more gladly about my weaknesses, so that Christ's power may rest on me. - 2 Corinthians 12:9

PONDER:

What false securities might the Father be asking you to release to Him? What do you need to receive instead?

DECLARATION:

Fear will no longer dictate my choices as I place my trust in God.

DAY 19

HOLD MY
WORDS CLOSELY

M Y CHILD, AS you follow Me into the new land I have for you, learn to hold My words to you very near. As you do, you will see My involvement, intervention and deliverance in an ever-increasing way.

You are not so different from the children of Israel who found themselves *marching out boldly*, following My presence into a land they had only heard and dreamed about. Pharaoh's army pursued and overtook them as the Israelites camped by the Red Sea.

You may have felt overtaken too, at times. It is in these times that you must hold My words to you closely. You are learning a greater dimension of walking by faith and not by sight.

My child, I want to be your default option. Hold fast to My words and when your back is up against a wall, watch for My deliverance. I will turn the enemy's plans around and ambush him just as I did with Pharaoh's army.

Yes, I have a turn-around and ambush of your enemies in store for you. Trust in Me and you will find that I have dry ground for you. Watch for the steadfast and unshakeable ground that I will give to you.

Stand firm, dear one. Yes, stand firm and you will see My salvation. You are gaining ground in the Spirit as you trust Me and move forward in faith. I will use your deliverance to display My glory to those around you.

The LORD hardened the heart of Pharaoh king of Egypt, so that he pursued the Israelites, who were marching out boldly. The Egyptians—all Pharaoh's horses and chariots, horsemen and troops—pursued the Israelites and overtook them as they camped by the sea near Pi Hahiroth, opposite Baal Zephon. - Exodus 14:8-9

Moses answered the people, "Do not be afraid. Stand firm and you will see the deliverance the

LORD will bring you today. The Egyptians you see today you will never see again. The LORD will fight for you; you need only to be still." - Exodus 14:13-14

PONDER:

Where are you in your journey of "taking your land"? What are His words to you as you move forward in faith?

DECLARATION:

I will stand firm and see the deliverance of My God!

LIVING FROM THE SECRET PLACE

M Y CHILD, I want to teach you how to live from a different place. I want to show you what it truly means to live from your secret place with me. There is a new level for you to ascend. It is a place of total peace, life, and joy. You can have joy right where your enemies dwell.

If you live with one foot in each world, both heaven and earth, you will experience some of both worlds. Why would you want to continue to experience fear, turmoil, and anxiety? Cast all your cares on Me and come up higher with Me. The storm can be raging all around you, but you will remain safe under My wings.

I'm calling you to a time of greater trust. It is called a *leap of faith* because it requires a total trust in My ability to catch you and lead you. This season is a time to intentionally yield and take a *trust walk* with Me.

Do you believe I will carefully lead you on the path? Can you trust Me to open doors for you? Can you trust Me to keep you from falling? Can you trust Me to equip and anoint you for what lies ahead?

The enemy has sought to weigh you down with worries, fears, and distractions. Hold fast to My voice and hold on to Me. Let go of all the weights and yield to the joy and mystery of the season and all that lies ahead.

When my heart was grieved and my spirit embittered, I was senseless and ignorant; I was a brute beast before you. Yet I am always with you; you hold me by my right hand. You guide me with your counsel, and afterward you will take me into glory. Whom have I in heaven but you? And earth has nothing I desire besides you. My flesh and my heart may fail, but God is the strength of my heart and my portion forever. - Psalms 73:21-26

Come to me, all you who are weary and

burdened, and I will give you rest. Take my yoke upon you and learn from me, for I am gentle and humble in heart, and you will find rest for your souls. For my yoke is easy and my burden is light. - Matthew 11:28-30

PONDER:

Where is God calling you into a "leap of faith" with Him? What weights can you release to Him today so that you might run unfettered?

DECLARATION:

I live from My secret place with God where there is life, hope, joy, peace, and love.

I AM YOUR DELIVERER

MY CHILD, I am calling you to set your gaze forward. I want to draw your attention away from the turbulent circumstances all around you and cause your faith to increase. I will deliver you from the enemies that pursue you. Please know that I have so much more than deliverance for you. You are being prepared for the *greater things* that have long been designated for this time. New places and new lands await you. Expansion of your gifts and callings await you.

When the enemy comes in to discourage, mock, or taunt you, it is time to hold up the standard of who I am, and what I have spoken to you. Trust in Me, and I will part the sea of impossibilities in your life. It is not a season to hesitate or doubt, but instead, fully abandon yourself to Me and resolutely march forward.

My child, I did not completely remove the waters of the Red Sea, but instead walled them up on either side so that Moses and the children of Israel could walk through on dry ground. I may not always remove your waters either, but I will provide a way through the obstacles that stand between you and the destiny I have prepared for you. I am your Deliverer.

I am calling you to a greater level of trusting, seeing, believing, and partnering with Me as you venture into new opportunities in the land I am giving you. Are there things in your heart that would keep you from fully giving Me your "Yes"? I am revealing the lies that have bound you. Release those things to Me and now receive My revelation.

I have equipped and empowered you for this next phase of your journey. It is not a time to be looking over your shoulder for the enemies who pursue, but instead a time of intentional forward movement. It is a time to see your season of "*exceedingly abundantly above all that you could ask or imagine*" unfold.

> Then the LORD said to Moses, "Why are you crying out to me? Tell the Israelites to move on. Raise your staff and stretch out your hand over

the seas to divide the water so that the Israelites can go through the sea on dry ground." Exodus 14:15-16

Then Moses stretched out his hand over the sea, and all that night the LORD drove the sea back with a strong east wind and turned it into dry land. The waters were divided, and the Israelites went through the sea on dry ground, with a wall of water on their right and on their left. Exodus 14:21-22

PONDER:

In what ways might God be stretching or expanding you in this season? What "greater things" do you long to see Him do in and through your life?

DECLARATION:

God has equipped and empowered me for the next phase of my journey.

SEE! THE WINTER IS PAST

Arise, my darling, my beautiful one, come with me. See! The winter is past; the rains are over and gone. Flowers appear on the earth; the season of singing has come, the cooing of doves is heard in our land.

SONG OF SONGS 2:10-12

MY WARM WINDS
ARE BLOWING

M Y CHILD, A new season is upon you! Can you sense the change in the air? The warm winds of My Spirit are beginning to blow and that which has seemed impossible will begin to occur.

Now your barren root will become a shoot! The dark hidden soil of your circumstances has covered My seeds of promise and you thought you would not experience their life again. But now, springing up like Ezekiel's dry bones, My seeds of promise are breathing and budding. I have ordained the life-changing winds this new season brings.

The surety of the rain that comes down from Heaven, watering the seeds and causing them to grow, is a sign for you of My never-ending faithfulness to watch over My words to perform them.

Yes, your barren root will become a shoot! It is time to sing over the barren places in your life. Let your faith be released through your song as you welcome in confident agreement the things I have spoken to you. Your worship, without yet seeing, unlocks the favor and resources of Heaven to move mountains. I will open up streams in the most unlikely barren places and abundant fruit where the vines have withered.

My child, as My warm winds blow, remain fixed on My presence. Move with Me, flow with Me, as you have never been this way before. Welcome with joy this season of fruitfulness and harvest, for all of creation has longed for this time.

"Sing, barren woman, you who never bore a child; burst into song, shout for joy, you who were never in labor; because more are the children of the desolate woman than of her who has a husband," says the LORD. – Isaiah 54:1

As the rain and the snow come down from heaven, and do not return to it without watering the earth and making it bud and flourish, so that it yields seed for the sower and bread for the eater, so is my word that goes out

*from my mouth; It will not return to me empty,
but will accomplish what I desire and achieve
the purpose for which I sent it. – Isaiah 55:10-11*

PONDER:

What areas of promise in your life are you watching for the early signs of new life to emerge? How can you welcome, with joy, the birthing of promised new things before they occur?

DECLARATION:

My God is able to bring life to the barren places around me.

DAY 23
LIFE WILL BURST FORTH

MY CHILD, THE enemy has sought to silence your voice, to snuff out what I am doing, but I will put My song in your mouth. As you partner with My Spirit, prophetic praises will erupt from your innermost being, declaring the things that are to come. This display of faith will have a ripple effect causing those around you to pause in wonder and believe.

I have not forgotten you or left you alone. Instead, I am covering you and watching over you and matters pertaining to you. You are a seed that I have planted. Though it seems sometimes that the seed has died and your vision with it, I will resurrect what seems to be dead. Out of this place of darkness, life will burst forth. New shoots of life will emerge.

See, I will do a new thing, an unexpected thing. Your time of silence will end, and you will find your voice again. You have sensed the season changing, and with it you will change, too. Can you feel My warm winds beginning to blow? The warm breath of My mouth will blow, melting the ice and chill away from things surrounding you. You will be amazed as that which lay hidden and cloaked in bitter cold, now emerges green, vibrant, and full of life.

I have been at work beneath it all, preparing an abundant harvest. It is time to awaken! Lift up your eyes to see what I am about to do. Fix your eyes forward and not behind, for I am doing a new thing.

Shake off the grave clothes of your former season. Like Lazarus coming out of the tomb that held him, you will come forth! You will come forth lighter, richer, deeper, and stronger. The death grip of the enemy has only served to make you stronger, and now you will come forth as My victorious one. I have abundance in store for you and My banquet table is prepared with the finest of fruit.

Jesus said to her, "Your brother will rise again."
Martha answered, "I know he will rise again in

the resurrection at the last day." Jesus said to her, "I am the resurrection and the life. The one who believes in me will live, even though they die; and whoever lives by believing in me will never die. Do you believe this?" - John 11:23-26

Then Jesus said, "Did I not tell you that if you believe, you will see the glory of God?" So they took away the stone. Then Jesus looked up and said, "Father, I thank you that you have heard me. I knew that you always hear me, but I said this for the benefit of the people standing here, that they may believe that you sent me." When he had said this, Jesus called in a loud voice, "Lazarus, come out!" The dead man came out, his hands and feet wrapped with strips of linen, and a cloth around his face. Jesus said to them, "Take off the grave clothes and let him go." - John 11:40-44

PONDER:

Ask Holy Spirit to help you identify if you might have any "grave clothes" from a former season that you need to leave behind. Now imagine pulling up your chair to His banquet table. What do you see, sense, feel, or experience there?

DECLARATION:

God will produce an abundant harvest through my life.

Day 24

New Garments for a New Season

M Y CHILD, YOU may have felt as if you are in a holding pattern, always circling and waiting to land in your land of promise. The seeds of My promises are planted within you and their birthing can take time. This waiting and longing for what you cannot yet see may have seemed intense, but you must remember that all My promises are yes and amen.

I am preparing you for the next phase of your journey and it is not in My heart for you to cut short the preparation process. I will not send you into your next assignment without training and preparing you with everything you will need. I have upgrades for you in this season. As we walk through this time together, keep your heart open to Me even when you don't see the way ahead of you. Guard your heart wellspring and linger in the secret place with Me.

The upgrades I have for you will enable you to see and know Me in a new way. You will understand who you are in a new way as well. I want to clothe you with new garments for the new season. Get rid of everything that weighs you down and entangles you, keeping you from embracing the new.

Don't be in a hurry, for *I* am not in a hurry. Joshua and the children of Israel surely expected to launch into setting up their homes after crossing into their promised land, however, I had a different plan. It was in this very place that I gave the order for Joshua to stop and circumcise all the men before moving forward. They had to pause and camp until everyone had healed.

It was in this pause that I rolled away the reproach of Egypt from My people. Though they had left Egypt a long time ago, they still carried the shame of Egypt in their hearts. They still felt like slaves and orphans in their hearts, though in reality they were free and loved. It was this act of My love that would cause them to leave the past behind.

I want to see you courageously and confidently step into your next assignment. Allow me to re-move any reproach or shame you might feel about the past, and receive the peace and assurance that will come as you freshly consecrate your heart to Me. Do not be discouraged in your holding pat-tern, for I am deeply at work.

> *And after the whole nation had been circumcised, they remained where they were in camp until they were healed. Then the LORD said to Joshua, "Today I have rolled away the reproach of Egypt from you." So the place has been called Gilgal to this day. – Joshua 5:8-9*

> *I delight greatly in the LORD; my soul rejoices in my God. For he has clothed me with garments of salvation and arrayed me in a robe of his righteousness, as a bridegroom adorns his head like a priest, and as a bride adorns herself with her jewels. – Isaiah 61:10*

PONDER:

Ask Holy Spirit to show you any lingering orphan thinking that needs to be left behind as you em-brace more fully your identity as a covenant son or daughter of God. Picture yourself removing the "old garments of orphanhood" and putting on your new garments of royal identity in Christ.

DECLARATION:
God is working all things together for my good.

DAY 25

I WILL BRING YOU THROUGH

M Y CHILD, YOU have often felt as if you are waiting for something, yet you could not see ahead. You have been in a spiritual birth canal, and I have given you the needed grace for the long wait and labor. You are coming out of your narrow place into a wide-open space. It is almost time for the revealing.

My season of preparation has served to shape and form you and make you ready to fully function by grace in the land I am giving you. Like a butterfly emerging from the tightly wound chrysalis, you will emerge with new wings, fashioned and formed for such a time as this.

The enemy has sought to abort the promises

I am birthing in you, but hold onto Me, and I will surely bring you through. My love is breaking open the way as you move by faith into this new season. It is a broad place that I have prepared for you. The discouragement, accusations, and hopelessness that you may have felt in the dark and narrow place are going to be exchanged for amazement and awe at My faithfulness in your life.

Just as the mother of a newborn quickly forgets the pain of childbirth as she enjoys the new life in her arms, so it will be, as this new season unfolds. You will be overcome in realizing the great love I have had for you all along.

Yes, I rescue you because I delight in you! You are going to know this in your heart and not just your head. I am rooting and grounding you in My love so that the storms and trials of life will no longer have the power to topple you or cause you to doubt My love for you.

> *When I was at my weakest, my enemies attacked—but the Lord held on to me. His love broke open the way and he brought me into a beautiful, broad place. He rescued me— because his delight is in me! – Psalm 18:18-19, TPT*

I will be glad and rejoice in your love, for you saw my affliction and knew the anguish of my soul. You have not given me into the hands of the enemy but have set my feet in a spacious place. – Psalm 31:7-8

PONDER:

Do you feel you have the heart knowledge that the Father delights in you? Today ask the Father to ground you more deeply in His love.

DECLARATION:

My time of preparation will produce greater fruitfulness in the next season.

DAY 26

I AM INTIMATELY INVOLVED

MY CHILD, I am in the *push!* Though your labor has often felt long and intense, it is never My desire to cause you pain. As your Father, I have the advantage to see what is on the other side of your birthing process. Your entire focus may often be on what is on the other side of the circumstances that hold you, but I am focused on your growth and maturity. It is My joy to see you mature fully, lacking nothing.

I will never forsake you. I am intimately involved in your process, overseeing every detail to make sure you emerge beautiful and powerful like the butterfly.

It is My joy to display My glory in and through

you. Only you can display the unique facets of My kingdom glory that you were created to display.

I am perfecting that which I started in you and will see the process through to see you emerge fully equipped and transformed for the assignments I have marked for you in this next season.

The enemy has taunted and mocked you with his lies. But, if you listen closely, the truth of My words, written upon your very heart shouts, "*You are blessed in the heavenly realms with every spiritual blessing in Christ.*" This you are, My beloved child.

I am watching over all things pertaining to you. The stage is set for your entrance into all I have prepared, and you will not arrive late.

> *...being confident of this, that he who began a good work in you will carry it on to completion until the day of Christ Jesus. -- Philippians 1:6*

> *Praise be to the God and Father of our Lord Jesus Christ, who has blessed us in the heavenly realms with every spiritual blessing in Christ. For he chose us in him before the creation of the world to be holy and blameless in his sight. — Ephesians 1:3-4*

PONDER:

If the enemy has taunted you with any lies concerning your destiny or future, take a moment and ask Holy Spirit for scriptures that reveal truth to you. Speak them out whenever the enemy attempts to lie to you.

DECLARATION:

I have a powerful destiny and God will display His glory through my life.

Day 27

My Promises Stand Firm

M Y CHILD, I am doing much in you and will surely bring to completion what I have begun. The enemy always opposes what I want to birth. He wants to abort the plans I have for revival and harvest, but do not fear, my promises stand firm.

My word reminds you, *"Do I bring to the moment of birth and not give delivery?" says the Lord."* *(Isa. 66:9)* You can be confident that My plans and purposes will prevail as you put your trust in Me.

It is time to prepare for what I am birthing around you and through you. Just as a newborn requires commitment, sacrifice, hard work, and lots of unconditional love, the things I am birthing will require these things and more. This will be a birthing full of My grace, and your steps of obedience will open the windows of Heaven. I want to lavish My favor and blessing on those things where you have sown and labored.

You have experienced a time of sifting, shifting, moving, and transition. You have known the intensity of the season. I am bringing all things into my fullness and using this pressure to bring about good in your life. I have not left you alone, but instead am overseeing every detail.

My child, don't take even a second to look behind you. I am doing a new thing. Just as I cut off the waters of the Jordan so that the children of Israel could cross, I will cut off the waters that threaten you. Instead, I will immerse you in *My* river. My Ezekiel 47 river will bring life to your dead circumstances. Everything *My* river touches comes to life.

It is a time of proliferation! See it spring up, signs of life everywhere!

Forget the former things; do not dwell on the past. See I am doing a new thing! Now it springs up; do you not perceive it? I am making a way in the desert and streams in the wasteland. — *Isa. 43:18-19*

Fruit trees of all kinds will grow on both banks

of the river. Their leaves will not wither, nor will their fruit fail. Every month they will bear fruit, because the water from the sanctuary flows to them. Their fruit will serve for food and their leaves for healing. —Ezekiel 47:12

PONDER:

What are some practical steps you can take to prepare for what God is birthing in and around you? What signs of "new life" are you seeing around you?

DECLARATION:

I will see new life in my circumstances as God immerses me in His river of life.

Day 28

Trust My Voice
and Character

M Y CHILD, I have heard your cries. You have
called out to me concerning your future and
passions, and I have heard your heart. Do not feel
that you must fit into a certain pattern or mold. My
kingdom is expansive, and My gifts are colorful
and diverse with different nuances for everyone.

I am building within you the very thing that
will make you feel fully alive. Don't be afraid to
move towards passion. Don't be afraid to be fully
you. You have felt the sting of mocking voices that
would say as they said to Me, *"Can anything good
come from Nazareth?"*

Now, set your face as flint and move forward
with Me. I have set doors before you and will open

them in My timing as you move forward with Me. Guard the purity of your heart and the purity of our relationship.

My heart is full of compassion for you and all you are encountering. Remember, I have not left you alone. Holy Spirit is inside of you to speak, comfort, and guide you every step of the way.

I am teaching you to trust My voice, but even greater, My character. I only give good gifts. This revelation knowledge of My goodness will lift heaviness from you and act as a compass on your journey into your destiny.

Your adversary is the father of lies. There is no truth in him at all. My grace is entirely sufficient for you. Keep your mind on things above and keep the gates locked that would allow the enemy to speak or gain any ground. I did not create your negative circumstances, but I will use them to propel you even further into your destiny. I am fine-tuning the things I have been building in you. Trust Me.

> *Because the Sovereign LORD helps me, I will not be disgraced. Therefore have I set my face like flint, and I know I will not be put to shame. He who vindicates me is near. Who then will bring charges against me? Let us face each other! Who is my accuser? Let him confront me! – Isaiah 50:7-8*

*I know your deeds. See, I have placed before you an open door that no one can shut. I know that you have little strength, yet you have kept my word and have not denied my name. –
Revelation 3:8*

PONDER:

Is there an area in your life where you have hesitated to move towards passion? Ask Father to reveal if there are any lies you might be believing. If so, repent, and ask for His perspective and strategies for moving forward.

DECLARATION:

I trust the voice of my Father to speak, guide, and direct my life.

BREAK THROUGH THE GATE AND GO OUT

The One who breaks open the way will go up before them; they will break through the gate and go out. Their King will pass through before them, the LORD at their head.

MICAH 2:13

I NURTURE AND PROTECT YOU

MY CHILD, IT is I who have hidden you. I carefully chose this place of obscurity for your growth and protection. Moses was placed in a papyrus basket of hiddenness, and I was present, hovering over his life to nurture this one who would one day lead My children out of slavery and into freedom.

Now, just as I did with Moses, I have nurtured and protected you. You were an embryo of destiny and look what My hands have formed in you! The seeds I planted in you have endured the storms, and bravely persisted through the harsh elements.

Like the kernel of wheat that must experience death to produce life, you are now a flourishing vine, and your leaves will bring nourishment and healing to others.

Be encouraged because your time of unveiling is near. You have allowed My process to shape, mold, and change you. You have resisted the urge to jump ship when the waves were tumultuous. You trusted me, and your courageous trust has brought joy to My heart.

The season is changing, dear one. I am releasing keys that will open doors before you. There is no stress or striving in what I have planned for you. My wind will move you forward into the new. My wind is at your back even now, moving, positioning, and propelling you into My more. Catch the wind, brave one. Catch the wind!

You will learn to ride the swells of My Spirit wind into new adventures with Me. Let go of fear, insecurity, and hesitation as these things have no place in what I have planned for you. Embrace the reality that I am doing a new thing. Embrace the change, for transition is in the air.

You have learned to trust Me in your hiddenness, now will you trust Me with your revealing? My glory is rising upon you. No longer will you be a hidden one, but My light on a hill. Rise up and step through your door into the new.

And we all, who with unveiled faces contemplate the Lord's glory, are being transformed into his image with ever-increasing glory, which comes from the Lord, who is the Spirit. — 2 Corinthians 3:18

Arise, shine, for your light has come, and the glory of the LORD rises upon you. See, darkness covers the earth and thick darkness is over the peoples, but the LORD rises upon you and his glory appears over you. – Isaiah 60:1-2

PONDER:

Do you have trouble turning the page into a new season with God? Today, release to Him any fears, insecurities, or hesitation. Take a deep breath and mentally step into the new.

DECLARATION:

The glory of God is rising upon me.

DAY 30

YOUR AUTHOR
AND FINISHER

M Y CHILD, I am pulling back the curtain on the play of your life to reveal how I have been at work. Yes, full circle moments are upon you! I am bringing full circle those things and situations in your life that caused you pain, despair, and heartache.

Dead dreams will now be brought back to life as I blow away the dust from the dark corners where they once seemed hidden and forgotten. Watch as some things that were once hidden in those corners now become center stage.

There will be so much joy as you experience the fulfillment of My promises. You will know in your deepest being that it is I who have done these things. I am truly working your *all things* together for good, just like I promised that I would.

The places where you laid down your life, your reputation, your hope for advancement, believing it may never be resurrected, I am breathing life, life, life now to show you I have not forgotten you. I have seen it all, and I have kept and cherished your tears, treasuring each one as a seed of what I knew that I would do.

Never forget that I am a *Finisher* of what I have started. I am the Author and Finisher of *your* faith. I will not leave your faith story unfinished as you place your trust in Me. I am writing and weaving a unique plot that brings Me great delight and glory.

O Lord, our God, no one can compare with you. Such wonderful works and miracles are all found with you! And you think of us all the time with your countless expressions of love—far exceeding our expectations! —Psalm 40:5(TPT)

For this reason, since the day we heard about you, we have not stopped praying for you. We continually ask God to fill you with the knowledge of his will through all the wisdom and understanding that the Spirit gives, so that you may live a life worthy of the Lord and please him in every way; bearing fruit in every good work, growing in the knowledge of God, being strengthened with all power according to his glorious might so that you may have great endurance and patience, and giving joyful thanks to the Father, who has qualified you to share in the inheritance of his holy people in the kingdom of light. –Colossians 1:9-12

PONDER:

Is there an area of life you laid down, or a "dead dream" that you sense the Holy Spirit wants to resurrect? Spend a moment allowing Him to breathe new life into those things. Write down any new plans or strategies He might give you.

DECLARATION:

God is releasing new life into areas that once seemed dead.

DAY 31

I AM TAKING YOU HIGHER

THE WALLS AND barriers that have kept you out of breakthrough are going to begin to fall as you move forward in faith and obedience to My voice. The enemy has sought to make you believe that the walls are too thick, or the barriers too high. You will see the walls fall down as you place your trust in Me.

My servant, David, found himself in a situation where he had lost everything. Even his own mighty men began to turn against him. But David had learned the secret of turning to Me to find his strength.

Will you lay down your own wisdom, your own methods, and simply turn to Me? As you turn to

Me in worship, I will shift your perspective. I will reveal to you My way of seeing. You will see with new eyes and comprehend from My viewpoint. It is in this place of worship that I will take you higher, up above the storms to release to you My plans for your breakthrough. This *hinge* of worship is the place where I can work and turn your life in a new direction. This is the place where My war room strategies and battle plans are given.

I have a plan for you to *pursue, overtake, and recover all* just as I did for David when he found himself facing the loss of everything he held dear. You will face your battles in My strength and return with plunder. That which has been stolen from you, I will restore to you seven-fold. The things the enemy has meant for evil in your life, I will turn for good because I love you, and you are My called one.

Step into the stream of grace from Heaven I am releasing for you. It is the stream of grace for breakthrough. It is a time of victory, vindication, and joy for you!

David recovered everything the Amalekites had taken, including his two wives. Nothing was missing: young or old, boy or girl, plunder or anything else they had taken. David brought everything back. He took all the flocks and herds, and his men drove them ahead of the other livestock, saying, "This is David's plunder."— I Samuel 30:18-20

For the Lord takes delight in his people; he crowns the humble with victory. Let his faithful people rejoice in this honor and sing for joy on their beds. May the praise of God be in their mouths and a double-edged sword in their hands, to inflict vengeance on the nations and punishment on the peoples, to bind their kings with fetters, their nobles with shackles of iron, to carry out the sentence written against them—this is the glory of all his faithful people. Praise the Lord. —Psalm 149:4-9

PONDER:

Do you have lost or stolen things that you would like to retrieve from the enemy's camp? If so, spend some time in worship and receive His grace and battle plans for retrieval and taking plunder.

DECLARATION:

God is giving me strategies for breakthrough that will bring me victory over the enemy.

DAY 32

POSITIONED IN
DEPENDENCE

MY CHILD, YOU have never been this way before. I spoke these same words to the children of Israel as they were preparing to cross into their promised land. You are crossing into your own promised land as well.

The Israelites were to keep their eyes on the Ark of the Covenant because it housed My very Presence. Now, My Presence resides *within* you. Now, tune in and turn aside to the gentle promptings of My voice.

You have felt the sting of impossibility taunting you as you face your own Jordan River at flood stage. Your circumstances have mocked My words to you, but you have turned to Me and leaned in close.

You are positioned now in a place of dependence, dear one. Here you will come to know Me as your True Savior, Deliverer, Fierce Champion, and Rescuer. Yes, trust in Me completely, and I will deliver you into your land.

The darkness around you has sought to hide My face from you. This is your place of rest and trust. I will be found faithful.

Yes, you have never been this way before. I have a steadfast path for you amid the raging waters. Rest in Me and you will see My goodness in the land of the living.

> *The water flowed back and covered the chariots and horsemen—the entire army of Pharaoh that had followed the Israelites into the sea. Not one of them survived. But the Israelites went through the sea on dry ground, with a wall of water on their right and on their left. –Exodus 14:28-29*

> *The LORD replied, "My Presence will go with you, and I will give you rest." Then Moses said to him, "If your Presence does not go with us, do not send us up from here. How will anyone know that you are pleased with me and with your people unless you go with us? What else will distinguish me and your people from all the*

other people on the face of the earth?" And the
LORD said to Moses, "I will do the very thing
you have asked, because I am pleased with you
and I know you by name."—Exodus 33:14-17

PONDER:

Have you known what it is like to be in a place of total dependence on God? What aspects of His name have been revealed to you in those places? Thank Him for how He reveals Himself to you when you most need Him.

DECLARATION:

I will not be overcome by impossibilities but
place my trust in God to deliver me.

Day 33

I Will Provide for You

MY CHILD, BE aware that breakthrough is possible at any time. I have powerful encounters waiting for you when you set your heart to hear and obey. Put your full trust in Me and obey My words and promptings.

I do not demand perfection of you, but I delight in lavishing My love and good gifts that are revealed for you on the pathway of obedience. Sometimes I conceal My breakthrough for a time so that you will experience an even greater measure of My glory.

My servant Abraham experienced Me as Jehovah Jireh, "The Lord Will Provide". This moment was a place of costly obedience for him. He chose to obey, and then when it seemed that all would be lost, My ram in the thicket was revealed.

Your encounters with Me will mark you, dear one. It is My joy to watch My glory manifest in and around you as you trust and wait for Me to move. Watch, wait, and believe for your breakthrough as I will provide your own *ram in the thicket*.

I am a promise keeping God. What I speak with My mouth I will do. You can always rely on My words as I am unable to lie.

You may feel as if you are being stretched too far, but you will find that you have a greater capacity than you thought. Launch it all out on me. My word will not return to you void. My word is never empty but will always accomplish what I sent it forth to do. Always!

Do not be afraid, for breakthrough is imminent. I have not given you a spirit of fear, so take heart and know that I am at work.

Then he reached out his hand and took the knife to slay his son. But the angel of the LORD called out to him from heaven, "Abraham! Abraham!" "Here I am," he replied. "Do not lay a hand on the boy," he said. "Do not do anything to him. Now I know that you fear God, because you have not withheld from me your son, your only son." Abraham looked up and there in a thicket he saw a ram caught by its horns. He went over and took the ram and sacrificed it as a burnt offering instead of his son. So Abraham called that place The LORD Will Provide..." Genesis 22:10-14

"Do not be afraid; you will not be put to shame. Do not fear disgrace; you will not be humiliated..." Isaiah 54:4a

PONDER:

Have you experienced a breakthrough in the past that felt as if it was delayed for a time? What aspect of God's character did He reveal to you in your waiting?

DECLARATION:

My God always keeps His promises.

DAY 34

ABBA'S SONG IN YOUR HEART

MY CHILD, I have positioned you for breakthrough. I have positioned you to be a *waymaker*. Like a runner in a race, you will break through the ribbon and step into new territory. It may be hard to comprehend now, but there will be many others who follow in your path of breakthrough. You are opening new territory in the Spirit realm each time you overcome, and others will greatly benefit.

The finish line is not the *finish*, but the beginning of new things. Focus! Keep your eyes on Me and you will go the distance with a grace that breaks off weariness as you run. Ignore the mocking voices from the sidelines that discourage saying, "*Failure, disappointment, and death to dreams.*" Meditate on My words and My promises.

Tune your heart to sing My praise and you will tap into My streams of mercy and the songs of Heaven. My song is a song of overcoming and victory.

My song in your heart will push you through. My song will shift your atmosphere and that of those around you. Do you hear it? It is a song of freedom! A song of deliverance! A song of breakthrough!

You must envision those who will stand in your breakthrough. You are fighting for more than yourself, but for your children, and their children, and for generations to come. The resistance you face is because you are shifting a path that will have the potential to change lives for generations.

My song in your heart will bring the breakthrough. It is Abba's song to you.

> "*Moses my servant is dead. Now then, you and all these people, get ready to cross the Jordan River into the land I am about to give to them--to the Israelites. I will give you every place where you set your foot, as I promised Moses.*"
> - Joshua 1:2-3

Then Miriam the prophet Aaron's sister, took a

timbrel in her hand and all the women followed her, with timbrels and dancing. Miriam sang to them: "Sing to the LORD, for he is highly exalted. Both horse and driver he has hurled into the sea." -- Exodus 15:20-21

PONDER:

What have been the words or the "mocking voices" that you have heard as you press toward your destiny and call? As you learn to recognize the enemy's voice, no longer give it a place of influence, but instead listen to Abba's song of love and victory over you.

DECLARATION:

My Father fights for me and will give me the strength to run my race.

I AM YOUR DADDY GOD

M Y CHILD, DO not be dismayed that you find strongholds of the enemy still inhabiting your promised land. Just as I had a specific plan for dismantling the walls and city of Jericho, I have a plan for you as well. The enemy's camp always appears fortified. He uses intimidation, lies, and false reports to try and cause you to recoil in fear.

Don't be surprised if the enemy's stronghold appears impenetrable. I will give you strategies to advance that may defy human reasoning and logic. My battle plans for Joshua involved marching, blowing ram's horns, and shouting. The faith of those who obeyed released My power to work and the walls were demolished as a result.

Sometimes your own logic and rational thoughts will be confronted by My strategies and plans. It is a time to align your heart and mind to receive from Me and obey what I am asking you to do.

The fatherless, or orphan, believes they must rely on themselves for their own survival or success. Come to Me, My beloved one, and know that I am your *Abba.* I am your *Daddy God* who loves you with an everlasting love. Know that I will fight for you.

Allow Me to heal and brush away any lingering orphan thinking from your heart and mind. There is true freedom and inheritance for you as you allow Me to touch the broken places that remain.

You will experience greater victory over the enemy's strongholds when you are fully aware and embrace My love for you. You are learning to war from a place of love, acceptance, and completed victory.

Now the gates of Jericho were securely barred because of the Israelites. No one went out and no one came in. Then the LORD said to Joshua, "See, I have delivered Jericho into your hands, along with its king and its fighting men. March around the city once with all the armed men. Do this for six days. Have seven priests carry trumpets of rams' horns in front of the ark. On the seventh day, march around the city seven times, with the priests blowing the trumpets. When you hear them sound a long blast on the trumpets, have the whole army give a loud shout; then the wall of the city will collapse and the army will go up, everyone straight in."—Joshua 6:1-5

What, then, shall we say in response to these things? If God is for us, who can be against us? He who did not spare his own Son, but gave him up for us all—how will he not also, along with him, graciously give us all things? — Romans 8:31-32

Ponder:

Have you often felt alone in fighting your battles? Today, release to Him your orphan thinking and receive His affirming declarations of love over your life.

Declaration:

Nothing can separate me from the love of God that is in Christ Jesus.

Week Six

Take Me Away with You— Let us Hurry!

Take me away with you—let us hurry! Let the king bring me into his chambers.

Song of Songs 1:4

Day 36

Come Sail with Me

M Y CHILD, YOU are headed into unchart- ed waters. There are no pre-made maps or charts to tell you where you are headed. Know that you are totally dependent on my voice to guide you in the unknown waters.

As we journey together, I have new adventures ahead for you. But you must untether your boat to launch out with me. I desire for you to move forward in faith with me, leaving the comfortable and familiar behind.

Are there weights in your boat that would slow you down and cause your vessel to falter, or even sink? Give to Me unforgiveness, control, fear of man, jealousy, and comparison. I will take these weights, and others, and throw them into the sea freeing you to travel unfettered.

Now relinquish what you have held onto instead of Me. These things are a false security, and they will hold you back from embracing the new. Yes, relinquish all to Me. You have sometimes wanted a glimpse of the new before you let go of the old, but I am asking you for a full relinquishing so that your yielded heart is free to fully embrace all that I have planned.

My child, it is time to step off the treadmill, where you have felt you are always stepping forward but never arriving anywhere new. Your full surrender will position you to encounter Me in ways you have hungered for and longed to experience.

Push past your fears, unanswered questions, past failures, and unbelief that have kept you tethered to the past season. You are moving into a new era of unprecedented breakthrough and freedom with Me. I am in your boat, My child, and together we will voyage into the new.

Therefore, since we are surrounded by such a great cloud of witnesses, let us throw off everything that hinders and the sin that so easily entangles. And let us run with perseverance the race marked out for us, fixing our eyes on Jesus, the pioneer and perfecter of faith. —Hebrews 12:1-2a

However, as it is written: "What no eye has seen, what no ear has heard, and what no human mind has conceived" --the things God has prepared for those who love him. —I Corinthians 2:9

PONDER:

How do you feel about the Father's invitation to join Him in new adventures? What are the things the Spirit is telling you to leave behind? What will you need for the journey?

DECLARATION:

I leave the past behind and trust the Father to walk with me into the new.

I AM UNDERLINING YOUR DESTINY

MY CHILD, YOU may have felt backed into a corner by the enemy. But it is in this corner that I will show Myself strong as you place all your hope and trust in Me. It is in this corner where the spirit of dread and intimidation will be overcome by the vindication and power of My Holy Spirit at work within you.

This spirit of dread and intimidation is a lying and bullying spirit. It feeds on the pathways of speculation where you have given it access. The goal of this spirit is to undermine your confidence and destiny and cut you off from the flow of My life-giving Spirit.

The enemy is seeking to undermine your destiny, but do not fear, for I am underlining your destiny. I am transforming you from one once cornered by dread, to My overcoming and fearless dread champion.

Shame and everlasting disgrace are the lot of your enemy as I made a public spectacle of him at the cross. There is coming for you a greater revelation and understanding of your place of victory as you are seated with Me in heavenly places.

Your enemy trembles at the thought of you believing and operating in this reality. Now, align yourself with truth.

As we move forward, your alignment with truth and all I have spoken to you is paramount. Tear down every argument that exalts itself against the knowledge of Christ. For, I have made you an overcomer.

> *No, in all these things we are more than conquerors through him who loved us. For I am convinced that neither death nor life, neither angels nor demons, neither the present nor the future, nor any powers, neither height nor depth, nor anything else in all creation, will be able to separate us from the love of God that is in Christ Jesus our Lord. –Romans 8:37-39*

And having disarmed the powers and authorities, he made a public spectacle of them, triumphing over them by the cross. — Colossians 2:15

PONDER:

Have you recently felt intimidated and under-mined by the enemy? Ask Jesus to give you His perspective from your seated place with Him. (You may want to journal the things He shows you.)

DECLARATION:

Satan has been defeated and disarmed because of Jesus' death and resurrection.

DAY 38

FOCUS ON ME

M Y CHILD, YOU are experiencing distractions all around you. The enemy wants to
cause you to lose traction and not be able to move
forward. If you focus on the distraction, you will
be stuck and unable to accomplish what I have for
you in this season. I have a place of traction for you
amid the distraction. Even when the very ground
beneath seems as if it is crumbling away, I have a
place for you to stand. I have ground for you to take
and I will give you what you need to move forward.

Distraction will often prevent you from giving
full attention to something else. Distraction seeks
to pull you off course. Therefore, your focus is ex-
tremely important right now. Though there may
be distractions of all types around, you can choose

how and what you will focus on. This journey of focus and finding traction in the midst of distraction will cause you to walk in a new level of authority even as warfare is all around you.

The enemy seeks to divert your eyes to the right or the left, deflecting your feet and attention from the path before you. My child, keep your eyes on Me and I will bring you through. I will give you strength and focus even as the chaos rages. You will be a lighthouse for others and a beacon amid swirling storms as you keep your gaze on Me and only Me.

I have miraculous solutions and provision for the mud pits you may find yourself stuck in. The very things the enemy used to cause you to be stuck, I will now use as stepping-stones to move you forward. Yes, though the enemy is saying, "You are losing ground," I am shouting, "We are gaining ground!" I am working beneath the surface in ways you cannot see to bring about the traction needed to propel you forward.

Let your eyes look straight ahead; fix your gaze directly before you."—Proverbs 4:25

The LORD is my shepherd, I lack nothing. He makes me lie down in green pastures, he leads me beside quiet waters, he refreshes my soul.

He guides me along the right paths for his name's sake. Even though I walk through the darkest valley, I will fear no evil, for you are with me; your rod and your staff, they comfort me. —Psalm 23:1-4

PONDER:

Is there an area where you have felt stuck or lost your traction? Ask Holy Spirit what distractions the enemy has used to divert your focus. With His leading, develop a strategy to move forward.

DECLARATION:

My focus is on My Father, and I am gaining ground.

Day 39

Trust Me in Your Freedom

MY CHILD, IT is time to come out of your foxhole. The time of hiding is coming to an end. You will lift your head and see that the smoke from your battlefield is clearing. You will be able to see again.

Now, I will clean and dress your battle wounds and give you food and drink. You have learned to trust me in your season of captivity, now will you trust me in your freedom?

I am removing your restraints and that which has held you back. Do not be afraid to run, My child. See, I am giving you eagle's wings and renewed strength. I have trained and equipped you to go the distance. Every trial that was sent to take you down, I am turning for your benefit and favor.

My child, get ready to run! Remember, you will run and not grow weary. Your connection to me, your *waiting* upon Me will supply the strength you need. There is a supernatural flow that you only receive as you *wait* upon Me.

I have called you to soar like an eagle, effortlessly gliding above the turmoil, stress, and anxiety that threatens you daily. As you drink from the fountain of My Presence you will not experience weariness. Drink from Me and run!

Do not fear that you will run backwards as I have set you in a season of forward motion. Don't be tempted to look behind, but throw off every weight, thought and hindrance to run the race that I have prepared for you. You will learn to ignore the jeers and taunts of the enemy from the sidelines, as he only wants to trip you up and slow you down. The former season has been about training you for the path ahead. You will need true mentors and significant community around you to hold up your arms. You have been equipped with what you need to run.

> *You prepare a table before me in the presence of my enemies. You anoint my head with oil; my cup overflows. Surely your goodness and*

*love will follow me all the days of my life, and
I will dwell in the house of the LORD forever.
—Psalm 23:5-6*

*Then the word of the LORD came to Elijah:
"Leave here, turn eastward and hide in the
Kerith Ravine, east of the Jordan. You will drink
from the brook, and I have directed the ravens
to supply you with food there." So he did what
the LORD had told him. He went to the Kerith
Ravine, east of the Jordan, and stayed there.
The ravens brought him bread and meat in the
morning and bread and meat in the evening,
and he drank from the brook. —I Kings 17:2-6*

PONDER:

Have you ever experienced a season of hiddenness or captivity? How did you learn to depend on
the Lord in that place? Ask Him for a shift in your
perspective today to see your new season through
eyes of faith and hope.

DECLARATION:

*I will run and not grow weary as I drink from
the fountain of His Presence.*

DAY 40

I AM OPENING
THE GATE

M Y CHILD, WE are in a time of great acceleration. You have known a time of rigorous conditioning and training like a racehorse. You have sometimes felt constrained and confined. Like the stalls that hold the racehorses before they are released, you have felt enclosed and shut in.

You have experienced frustrating delays, roadblocks, and hindrances. You have heard My words to you and believed Me and have felt bewildered and disappointed in the delays.

Today, I say to you, I will open the gate to your stall! The doors that have confined you will no longer hold you back. I am releasing you, My own racehorse to run the race marked out for you. You have been trained for such a time as this.

The sacrifices, the conditioning, the tedious laps you have endured have prepared you for the course ahead. You will now run swiftly and skillfully, completely in tune to the slightest tug on the reins from My hand. For, I have honed the hearts of My racehorses. I have honed your heart to beat like Mine. Because your heart is totally Mine, we will now run as one.

My child, as I open the gates, wait on My timing and run fully submitted to Me. The strength for this race must be My supernatural strength flowing through you.

Now give to Me your frustrations, fears, and disappointments. Allow your heart to move towards gratefulness for the things you have endured in preparation. My loving hand has prepared you to skillfully run.

Do you not know that in a race all the runners run, but only one gets the prize? Everyone who competes in the games goes into strict training. They do it to get a crown that will not last, but we do it to get a crown that will last forever. – I Corinthians 9:24-25

Those who belong to Christ Jesus have crucified the flesh with its passions and desires. Since we live by the Spirit, let us keep in step with the Spirit. —Galatians 5:24-25

PONDER:

Do you feel you have experienced a time of preparation for the race ahead of you? Spend some time thanking God for how He has trained and prepared you, expressing your desire to run as one with Him.

DECLARATION:

I will run the race ahead submitted to the Spirit of God.

Day 41

Sync with My Time

M Y CHILD, I am calling you to sync with My time. Do you not set your watch so that you will arrive on time? I am calling you to sync with *My* time so that you will arrive on time for the things I have called you to in this season.

I am issuing a wakeup call to My Church. It is time to be fully awake, alert, and aware of My timing and how I am moving. We are entering a *Kairos* time, a fullness of time season where I am bringing things together to fulfill My words and promises.

There have been many distractions in the past season, and I am urging you to yoke yourself to Me. When you are yoked, you will avoid the pitfalls and loss of traction that occurs as a result of walking alone. The enemy has sought to dull your hearing so that you move out of sync with Me. Be alert and aware that it is a time to be watchful and in tune with Me. Clear out the things that would cause your hearing to be hindered.

Step into the place I have for you. You are not alone in your journey, and you must not try to walk alone. Is not our journey together a place of trust? Trust and obey, and you will find My grace there to accompany you every step of the way.

Distractions have sought to rob you of destiny moments but aligning with Me will bring the necessary course corrections. As you sync with My time you will feel the freedom, exhilaration, rest, and deep fulfillment for which you were created. Awaken and lift up your eyes to see and experience My Kairos time, and together we will see the great harvest of the nations.

> Come to me, all you who are weary and burdened, and I will give your rest. Take my yoke upon you and learn from me, for I am gentle and humble in heart and you will find rest for your souls. For my yoke is easy and my burden is light. --Matthew 11:28-30

> Don't you have a saying, "it's still four months until harvest"? I tell you, open your eyes and look at the fields! They are ripe for harvest. — John 4:35

PONDER:

Have you known hindrances to hearing Him in this past season? What things might the Spirit be asking you to set aside in order to be in sync as you move forward?

DECLARATION:

I set aside every hindrance so that I can run the race well.

SEE WITH EYES OF FAITH

MY CHILD, I am not a man that I can lie. You are living in a time of great decisions and choices. Like Caleb, Joshua, and the ones sent in to spy out the land, you are able to survey the promised land before you. What will you decide? What will you perceive? Will you see the giants as insurmountable, or will you see with eyes of faith?

I have spoken. What will you now believe? I am calling you to run with Me in this faith journey. You cannot arrive at your decisions based on mere human logic and reasoning. I am calling you to something higher and greater. Your faith is the actual substance of things you have hoped for in Me.

In this journey with Me, you will live by every word that proceeds from My mouth. As you stay the course and put My word to the test, you will experience deep satisfaction and the fruit of My Spirit.

Others may scoff at you, and call you childish, foolish, and irrational. These would put Me in a box of convenience and predictability, as they arrive at decisions through man's best attempts at wisdom. This false wisdom falls short of what I have called you to, My child. You are made for more, and it is those who lay their fears aside, stepping fully into this journey of faith with Me, that will experience the exhilarating joy of this adventure.

Remember, you are surrounded by the great cloud of witnesses. These men and women, heroic in their faith, set their hearts on pilgrimage. I am calling you to do the same. Will you come with Me?

> *Brothers and sisters, I do not consider myself yet to have taken hold of it. But one thing I do: Forgetting what is behind and straining toward what is ahead, I press on toward the goal to win the prize for which God has called me heavenward in Christ Jesus. - Phil. 3:13-14*

> *Blessed are those whose strength is in you, who*

have set their hearts on pilgrimage. As they pass through the Valley of Baca, they make it a place of springs; the autumn rains also cover it with pools. They go from strength to strength, till each appears before God in Zion. —Psalm 84:5-7

PONDER:

As you see the land God has promised you, do you tend to see the giants, or do you believe what God has spoken to you? Today, ask Holy Spirit to reveal any hindrances to childlike faith in your life. If He reveals something to you, repent and ask for His perspective and change in your heart.

DECLARATION:

I have set my heart on pilgrimage with God and believe He will bring me into my promised land with Him.

A ROYAL DIADEM IN GOD'S HAND

You will be a crown of splendor in the LORD's hand, a royal diadem in the hand of your God.

ISAIAH 62:3

Day 43

Your Time of Commissioning

M Y CHILD, YOU are in a time of great awakening. I am raising up My army, My Royal Priests, clothed in righteousness and armed with revelation that has been warred over in the trenches of the former seasons.

The enemy has sought to destroy and remove your crown. His plan has been to discredit, demoralize, and disrobe you. But My awakening Spirit is upon you, and nothing can stop what I have ordained for this time. All of creation has longed for this time when you, My sons and daughters, arise into your call and place of authority.

You are an orphan no more! Your true birthright, identity, and inheritance I have revealed. A roar is going to come from deep within you as all I have put within you rises to the surface. You, My Royal Priests, are beginning to rise and the enemy trembles at the sound of your voice.

It is time for My Royal Priests to execute My vengeance and justice to the enemies of My kingdom. You will release chain breaking decrees and earth-shaking declarations that release freedom, healing, and deliverance. You are My chosen one, My treasure, and it is My delight to see you step fully into all I have called you to.

You are one of My Mordecai and Esther generation. You have not bowed your knee to any other and now I am commissioning you for such a time as this. You have been hidden, but now I am bringing you into the light. You are My beloved child, perfectly positioned to serve as one of My Royal Priests, releasing royal decrees and governmental edicts that change the course of nations.

I have extended My scepter of favor towards you. Now steward My favor with the utmost honor and humility, for I have entrusted it to you for the good of others.

> *But you are a chosen people, a royal priesthood, a holy nation, God's special possession, that you may declare the praises of him who called*

you out of darkness into his wonderful light. – I Peter 2:9

When he saw Queen Esther standing in the court, he was pleased with her and held out to her the gold scepter that was in his hand. So Esther approached and touched the tip of the scepter. Then the king asked, "What is your request? Even up to half the kingdom, it will be given you." – Esther 5:2-3

PONDER:

Have you understood that you are God's special possession? Have you known that His favor on you is for the good of others? As you pray today, commit the favor in your life to Him to see His kingdom advance. Ask for an increase of His favor, and wisdom to steward it well.

DECLARATION:

I am God's special possession so that I may declare the praises of Him who called me out of darkness into his wonderful light.

DAY 44

MY OAK OF RIGHTEOUSNESS

M Y CHILD, YOU have been in a season of great challenges, but I am breathing hope into you again. You have sometimes felt like the captives in Psalms 137 who mourned for the days of joy they once knew in Zion. You will once again experience joy and know the taste of My freedom. I am blowing away the dust and cobwebs from your dreams that were placed on the shelf.

I am breaking off any remaining traces of the orphan spirit and releasing my deep abiding sonship. The lie that you are alone and abandoned will be broken once and for all. You will know what it is to carry My heart again. You will be My dispenser of hope. You have sown in tears and NOW is the time of joyful reaping.

Your testimony will be a light for many. Your perseverance through the dark night is now releasing a beacon of hope for other captives. You must rise up and shine, My dispenser of hope!

You will lift up your eyes and see that the nations are coming to you. I have given you, My child, the keys to the Kingdom. I have given you authority to open and shut things. Take your place now at the gates. Take your place at the gates My oak of righteousness. Your branches will spread over cities and nations providing shade and protection for the lost and broken. The fruit of your limbs will sustain the weak and hungry, and your leaves will provide healing for the nations.

You are My planting. Rise and shine My dispenser of hope for you will display My splendor. This is your time to shine!

By the rivers of Babylon we sat and wept when we remembered Zion. There on the poplars we hung our harps, for there our captors asked us for songs, our tormentors demanded songs of joy they said, "Sing us one of the songs of Zion!" – Psalm 137:1-3

I will not leave you as orphans; I will come to you. Before long, the world will not see me

anymore, but you will see me. Because I live,
you also will live. On that day you will realize
that I am in my Father, and you are in me, and
I am in you. – John 14:18-20

PONDER:

Today, receive a fresh awakening in your spirit of His gift of sonship to you. Allow Holy Spirit to identify and blow away any remaining traces of the orphan spirit. Then, ask Holy Spirit for an assignment to release hope to someone today.

DECLARATION:

God has given me keys and authority to open
and shut things.

Day 45

Come Dream with Me

My CHILD, I am inviting you to dream again. I am inviting you to step out of a time of unfulfilled dreams and captivity into a new place of possibility and trust in My love for you. I am the One who can make water gush forth in the wilderness and burning sand become a pool.

I want to turn your mourning into dancing once again. I want to breathe life into the dreams of your heart. Even now, can you hear My Spirit whisper to your heart, *"Can these dreams live?"* What will be your answer?

It was in your place of captivity that you ceased to dream. I have set you free, dear one, and now you are free to dream with Me. The pain of your past caused you to stop seeing the possibilities of your present. Release to Me your *slave* mentality and the poverty thinking that has taken up residence. Though you are bought with a great price, I have given you abundant freedom in My kingdom. Now you are a slave to righteousness and forever My child and co-heir with My Son, Jesus. It is in this place of delightful belonging that dreams are created and birthed.

Some of your limitations have been imposed by others, and others are self-inflicted. Now I am erasing and removing your barriers. Remember, I am the One who parted the Red Sea. Allow Me to enlarge the borders of your faith and thinking. Allow Me to rewrite the *rules* for your next season. I am uncapping the wells of your dreams.

Come and fly with Me and I will teach you how to ride the wind. This is a place of height. This is a place above weariness and fainting. Trust in Me as the path I have ordained for you will sometimes not make sense. You will be called to do things that seem impossible, but I am with you. Wait and hope in Me and trust in My goodness.

> *When the Lord restored the fortunes of Zion, we were like those who dreamed. Our mouths were filled with laughter, our tongues with songs of joy. Then it was said among the nations, "The LORD has done great things for them."- Psalm 126:1-2*

Now to him who is able to do immeasurably more than all we ask or imagine, according to his power that is at work within us, to him be glory in the church and in Christ Jesus throughout all generations, forever and ever! Amen. - Ephesians 3:20-21

PONDER:

Repent of any self-inflicted limitations or poverty thinking that has affected how you dream with God. Release any slave thinking and receive your true sonship in Him. How does the reality that you are co-heirs with Christ affect your ability to dream?

DECLARATION:

I am free to dream and create as a beloved child of God.

RAISE YOUR EXPECTATIONS

M Y CHILD, AS you begin walking and exploring the new land I am giving you, it is important to remember that you now walk in new levels of increase and abundance. As the limitations of your former seasons fall away, your expectations need to rise to receive and utilize the grace I am pouring out.

Remember, the manna stopped when the Israelites came into their new land. They were no longer limited to what they had experienced as sustenance for so many years. I faithfully sustained them in their *narrow place*, but this was by no means all I had planned for them. They were now in the land of milk and honey with abundant fruits and vegetables to enjoy. How sad it would have been if they had continued to forage the ground, searching for the monotonous manna. They would have missed the abundant flavors, colors, and tastes of the extravagant foods I had placed for them in the new land.

My child, this is why I encourage you to lift your eyes and raise your expectations. Remove the lens with which you viewed your former season. You are stepping into a wide-open space I have prepared for you and there will be many changes. It will be an exhilarating journey of faith and trust as together with Me you step out into your new uncharted territory.

The stage has been set, and I have prepared every detail for this time. You have been waiting, backstage in your *narrow place*, often unable to see or even hear what is happening on the other side of the curtain. In My time, I will pull back the curtain on your life and reveal what I have been preparing in you all along.

The day after the Passover, that very day, they ate some of the produce of the land: unleavened bread and roasted grain. The manna stopped the day after they ate this food from the land; there was no longer any manna for the

Israelites, but that year they ate the produce of Canaan. - Joshua 5:11-12

The LORD will keep you from all harm--he will watch over your life; the LORD will watch over your coming and going both now and forevermore. - Psalm 121: 7-8

PONDER:

Is there an area of small or limited thinking you need to leave behind as you journey into the land God has for you? As you step into a new level of your faith journey with God, what would you like to receive from Him today to strengthen you? Ask, and then receive by faith what you need.

DECLARATION:

God will give me every place I set my foot as I take new territory for His kingdom.

Day 47

I am Enlarging You

MY CHILD, SURRENDER, release, and obey. Fear is not your portion, but instead, joy. I give deep abiding joy as you learn to trust in My goodness.

I am calling you to take new land and conquer giants. Your operating system will be *"not by might, nor by power, but by My Spirit." (Zech. 4:6)* Under the Old Covenant, the Israelites walked for forty years with sandals and clothing that did not wear out. I provided the nourishing manna for them daily. How much more under My glorious New Covenant will I provide for you! Surrender to Me your needs for I know them already. Release to Me the paths of small thinking and walk with Me on this new journey of intimacy and adventure.

I am enlarging you. Heed My voice quickly and you will avoid unnecessary delays. Remember, My kingdom is within you. Draw from this place and the way will open before you. You are pioneering and treading on unworn paths as My kingdom is ever advancing.

Don't let the familiar pull you away from the new. It is time for the new! New beginnings, new assignments, new lands, and new operating systems.

Fear has no place in this new era. I'm calling you to rise above and soar like the eagle. Renew your strength in Me and you will find supernatural grace for all I have called you to do.

Enlarge the place of your tent, stretch your tent curtains wide, do not hold back; lengthen your cords, strengthen your stakes. For you will spread out to the right and to the left; your descendants will dispossess nations and settle in their desolate cities. Do not be afraid; you will not be put to shame. Do not fear disgrace; you will not be humiliated. – Isaiah 54:2-4a

Therefore I tell you, do not worry about your life, what you will eat or drink; or about your body, what you will wear. Is not life more than food, and the body more than clothes? Look at the birds of the air; they do not sow or reap or store away in barns, and yet your

heavenly Father feeds them. Are you not much more
valuable than they? - Matthew 6:25-26

PONDER:

Have you realized your total dependence on God?
Do you know Him as your Provider, Sustainer,
Shepherd, and Lord? Meditate on each of these
names with Holy Spirit and embrace the encounters and upgrades He has for you.

DECLARATION:

I don't ever need to fear because God is forever
with me.

DAY 48

YOU ARE MY DESTINED ONE

M Y CHILD, AWAKEN to My voice and rise from your sleep. Sound the trumpet and the ram's horn for My glory is rising on you. It is I who have created and formed you. You are My destined one--born for such a time as this. Lift up your eyes to see that My fields are white unto harvest. I have lovingly sown and tended, and now I call you, My harvester, to come.

It is an *all-hands-on deck* time for My people. Now arise, My oak of righteousness, for your glory is now for the glory of the nations. Do not sow sparingly, but lavishly give as you have been lavishly given unto.

Welcome all My people. Welcome the orphan,

the widow, the sick, the rich, the poor, the outcast, and the star. All have a seat at My table. Break the bread of fellowship and drink the new wine of covenant.

It is time now to rebuild the ancient ruins. It is time to restore those places that have been devastated for generations. I have given to you My kingdom, and now you must take it and share it with others. Enforce the rule of the kingdom of light, My royal heir, for you have been chosen, appointed, commissioned, and anointed.

Put My decrees and declarations in your mouth, for they will bring Heaven to Earth, and light into darkness. I have seated you with Me in heavenly places. Now release the verdict of Heaven's court over My people. Forgiven! Healed! Delivered! Chosen! Empowered!

Lift up your eyes, My Bride. The fields are waiting, and the time is now.

The nations will see your vindication, and all kings your glory; you will be called by a new name that the mouth of the LORD will bestow. You will be a crown of splendor in the LORD'S hand, a royal diadem in the hand of God. - Isaiah 62:2-3

The LORD has made proclamation to the ends
of the earth: "Say to Daughter Zion, 'See, your
Savior comes! See, his reward is with him, and
his recompense accompanies him.. -Isaiah 62:11

PONDER:

Have you seen yourself as a "harvester" and one
who can restore places that have been devastated? Spend some time today receiving His call and
commissioning on your life for His eternal kingdom.

DECLARATION:

I am awakening to My call as one of the King's
royal heirs to release His heart of redemption
and restoration.

DAY 49

MY AWAKENED WARRIOR

M Y CHILD, YOUR heart has been awakened by the fiery passion and love of Jesus Christ, My Son. You are My warrior and part of My Bridal Army that I am awakening in this hour to go forth in My name. My awakened army will do great exploits that flow from a heart of love, purity, honor, and intimacy with Me.

I am calling you now to walk in alignment with the flow from Heaven. Those who hear My call and choose to obey will begin walking in an ever-increasing momentum as they march in synchronization with Me.

I want to be the central and dominant theme in your life. Every other influence must take a lesser

222 | *Sylvia Neusch*

place. This is the alignment that must take place for My authority to manifest through you.

Jesus Christ is the plumb line, and He is the precious cornerstone. I am building things upon Him as the one true foundation. You are also one of my *stones* being built into a spiritual house. You are one of My royal priesthood. I have set you apart as one who will proclaim My goodness and represent Me to the world.

Yes, you are a royal diadem in My hand, dear one. You are a beautifully jeweled crown to Me. I have redeemed you, restored you, and set you in a place of intimacy and authority with Me. You are an extension of My goodness and a picture of My unconditional and redemptive love to the world. I have called you by a new name and delight in who you are and who I have called you to be.

Rise up My bridal warrior. Rise up and take your place in My army of laid down lovers.

Since, then, you have been raised with Christ, set your hearts on things above, where Christ is, seated at the right hand of God. Set your minds on things above, not on earthly things. For you died, and your life is now hidden with Christ in God.- Colossians 3:1-3

And they sang a new song, saying: "You are worthy to take the scroll and to open its seals, because you were slain, and with your blood you purchased for God persons from every tribe and language and people and nation. You have made them to be a kingdom and priests to serve our God, and they will reign on the earth." - Revelation 5:9-10

PONDER:

You have learned and experienced many things on your journey with God so far. What are the memorial stones in your own life like the Children of Israel erected, that speak of your special encounters with God? Let them lead you to a place of gratefulness today.

DECLARATION:

I am a treasured possession of my Father God.

ABOUT THE AUTHOR

SYLVIA NEUSCH is a wife, mother, pastor, author, prophetic voice and prophetic blogger. Sylvia operates with an anointing to sense the times and seasons, exhorting the Body of Christ in stewarding the current and coming moves of God. Through her writing and teaching, Sylvia encourages and equips people to discover their own deep connection with God, and to enjoy their journey and process of growth with Him. Sylvia and her husband, Richard, are the senior leaders of True Life, a non-denominational church in Round Rock, Texas. They are also the founders and overseers of the Austin School of Supernatural Ministry. Sylvia and Richard have two adult children and four grandchildren.

www.ingramcontent.com/pod-product-compliance
Lightning Source LLC
LaVergne TN
LVHW022322080426
835508LV00041B/1744